YOU SHOULD MEET

Lin-Manuel Miranda

by Laurie Calkhoven

illustrated by Alyssa Petersen

Ready-to-Read

Simon Spotlight

New York London Toronto Sydney New Delhi

SIMON SPOTLIGHT
An imprint of Simon & Schuster Children's Publishing Division
1230 Avenue of the Americas, New York, New York 10020
This Simon Spotlight edition August 2020
Text copyright © 2018 by Simon & Schuster, Inc.
Illustrations copyright © 2018 by Alyssa Petersen
All rights reserved, including the right of reproduction in whole or in part in any form.
SIMON SPOTLIGHT, READY-TO-READ, and colophon are registered trademarks of Simon & Schuster, Inc.
Manufactured in China 0620 LEO

CONTENTS

Introduction

Have you ever dreamed about writing songs? Or about singing on the Broadway stage? How about making movies? Maybe you enjoy watching and listening to other people act and sing. Or maybe you want to spend your life singing and dancing and making people happy.

If you like to do any of those things, you should meet Lin-Manuel Miranda.

Lin-Manuel wrote *Hamilton*, one of the most popular Broadway musicals of all time. He also inspired people all over the world to learn about the beginnings of the United States of America. He taught the world about Latin music and Latino traditions. And he didn't do it overnight or by himself. Lin-Manuel spent many years working on his music and learning his craft. He also had a strong team of friends who helped him.

Lin-Manuel made his dreams come true. Once you meet him, no matter what you dream of doing, you'll be inspired to make your dreams come true too.

Chapter 1
New York Dreams

Lin-Manuel Miranda was born on January 16, 1980, in New York City. His parents, Luz Towns-Miranda and Luis A. Miranda Jr., were both from Puerto Rico. Puerto Rico is a part of the United States, but it is not a state. Lin-Manuel grew up in a mostly Hispanic neighborhood. His home was full of music. Lin-Manuel started learning to play piano when he was six. His parents listened to Spanish songs and Broadway show tunes. His older sister, also named Luz, liked hip-hop.

"You'd hear all kinds of different music coming out of car windows and storefronts and fire escapes," Lin-Manuel said about his neighborhood. He gives his sister, Luz, the credit for his good taste in music. "All of my first hip-hop albums were stolen from her." She also helped him get ready for the very first time he was on stage—at the kindergarten talent show. (He sang a song, of course!)

Lin-Manuel's parents worked very hard, but the family didn't have money to see Broadway shows. They bought the cast albums instead. Lin-Manuel would listen to them over and over to memorize the lyrics. He also loved Disney movies like *Beauty and the Beast* and *The Lion King*.

Lin-Manuel's favorite film was *The Little Mermaid*, and he loved the funny crab character named Sebastian. He went to see the movie many times. In the fourth grade, he used to jump up on his desk at school and sing Sebastian's song "Under the Sea." He also memorized the dance moves. The Disney movies even inspired Lin-Manuel to make his own recordings and videos.

Lin-Manuel went to a school for gifted children in New York City. A school for gifted children is a school for extraordinarily smart kids. Lin-Manuel has talked about how happy he was to share Puerto Rican culture with his classmates. He shared exciting Latin music and delicious food.

Even though he was very smart, Lin-Manuel was still a bit intimidated by his classmates. He felt like they were all smarter than he was. So he decided to pick something he wanted to do and work really hard at it. That was singing, acting, and writing songs. By the sixth grade, he was in all the school musicals.

In high school, Lin-Manuel was in almost every school play. He wrote plays and musicals of his own, which showed his classmates what it was like to be Puerto Rican. Lin-Manuel felt he had two choices. He could try to blend in, or he could try to stand out. He decided to stand out and make sure everyone knew he loved his Latino background.

Lin-Manuel also directed the show *West Side Story* in his senior year. The musical is about Puerto Rican and white teenagers in New York City who fight when a white boy falls in love with a Puerto Rican girl.

It wasn't just being Latino that made Lin-Manuel stand out. Everyone could see how talented he was. When it was time to go to college, he knew he would study musical theater. Lin-Manuel had a lot of dreams, but working in musical theater was the thing he most wanted to do.

Chapter 2
In the Heights

Lin-Manuel went to Wesleyan University in Connecticut to study theater arts. He performed in college musicals and wrote his own songs and shows. One of those shows was set in a Hispanic neighborhood near the one where Lin-Manuel grew up in New York City—Washington Heights. When he graduated college, he had a first draft of a musical called *In the Heights*. The show used Latin music and hip-hop to tell a story about the joys and troubles of the people in the neighborhood.

One week after he graduated from college, Lin-Manuel met with a friend from Wesleyan, Tommy Kail. Tommy was a theater director and thought *In the Heights* had promise. He encouraged Lin-Manuel to keep working on it and helped where he could. Other friends wanted them to meet a musician named Alex Lacamoire, who ended up joining them as the show's musical director.

While they were working on *In the Heights*, Lin-Manuel and Tommy also sang and acted with a hip-hop comedy group he had started in college called Freestyle Love Supreme. Audience members would shout out words, and Lin-Manuel and his friends would make up funny songs and skits. He wrote songs and acted in shows like *Sesame Street* and *The Electric Company*, and he also worked as a substitute teacher.

With Tommy as director, Alex as musical director, and Lin-Manuel in the lead role, *In the Heights* opened in a theater off-Broadway in 2007. Off-Broadway theaters are usually smaller than Broadway theaters.

In the Heights was a hit and moved to Broadway in 2008. It went on to win the Tony Award—the highest award a Broadway show can win—for Best Musical of the year. The cast recording won a Grammy Award.

Lin-Manuel's Broadway dreams were coming true. He continued to work on other shows, including a Spanish/English version of *West Side Story*, while he wondered what his next big project would be. Then one day he bought a biography of one of the United States founding fathers to read while he was on vacation. That biography of Alexander Hamilton would change his life.

Chapter 3
Hamilton's Beginnings

Lin-Manuel read about Alexander Hamilton's life while sitting by the pool at a hotel in Mexico. After just a few chapters, he realized that Hamilton would make a great subject for for a music album. Hamilton was a poor orphan from an island who came to America by himself. Hamilton then went on to become George Washington's right-hand man and a leader in the new country.

Lin-Manuel could relate to the story because his parents were poor and also came to the mainland U.S.

Lin-Manuel thought that hip-hop was the perfect music to tell Hamilton's story. Hip-hop music is filled with energy and excitement. So were the thirteen American colonies and the people who fought for independence from England.

Lin-Manuel had finished one song about Hamilton when he was invited to perform at the White House on May 12, 2009. President Barack Obama asked Lin-Manuel to sing a song from *In the Heights*, which was still on Broadway. Instead, Lin-Manuel decided to take a chance and try something

new. With Alex Lacamoire on the piano, Lin-Manuel sang about a poor immigrant who helped make America rich and strong. He sang "Alexander Hamilton," the song that would later be the opening number of the Broadway show.

The audience loved the song. President Obama was the first one on his feet to cheer. Millions of people watched Lin-Manuel sing the song on YouTube. Suddenly, the world wanted to know more about Alexander Hamilton—both the man and the album Lin-Manuel was working on.

For the next two years, Lin-Manuel was busy with other projects. Then, in June 2011, he sang "My Shot," the third song from the show, at a benefit performance. It had taken him more than a year to get the song exactly right.

The audience loved it. It was time for Lin-Manuel to get busy and write more songs.

Chapter 4
Broadway Bound

During the next three years, Lin-Manuel worked on *Hamilton* whenever he could. He also married Vanessa Nadal, a scientist and a lawyer. He first met Vanessa in high school. Lin-Manuel was too shy to talk to her then, but he found her on Facebook after college. He invited her to a Freestyle Love Supreme show and Vanessa went. Lin-Manuel was still too shy to talk to her that night, but a friend got her phone number for him. Vanessa came to more shows, and they started dating. They were married in 2010.

Vanessa and Lin-Manuel adopted a stray dog they found on a beach in the Dominican Republic. The half-starved dog nibbled on Vanessa's ankle. They decided to take the dog home and named her Tobillo, which is Spanish for "ankle." Today, they have two sons, Sebastian and Francisco. One of the reasons they named their first son Sebastian was because of the funny crab from *The Little Mermaid*!

All along, even after Lin-Manuel got married, he was still working on *Hamilton*. With the help of friends like Tommy and Alex, the show was ready to open at an off-Broadway theater in January 2015. Lin-Manuel played Alexander Hamilton.

Some people were surprised that Lin-Manuel chose people of color to play many of the leading roles. Historically, the people the roles were based on had been white. But Lin-Manuel thought it was important for the cast to look like America today, not the America of two hundred years ago. He also wanted to celebrate the people of color who helped build the United States and didn't get credit in history books.

The show ended up being a huge success off-Broadway and moved to Broadway in July 2015, to the same theater where *In the Heights* played. (The theater is almost directly across the Hudson River from the spot where, in real life, Alexander Hamilton was shot by Aaron Burr in a duel in 1804.)

Hamilton was greeted by fireworks over the Hudson on opening night. It won the Pulitzer Prize for Drama and won eleven Tony Awards, including Best Musical. Lin-Manuel's friends Tommy and Alex also won Tony awards.

In July 2016, Lin-Manuel made his final appearance in the show. But *Hamilton* continues to break records on Broadway and beyond with shows opening in other cities around the country and even in London, England.

Chapter 5
Reaching New Heights

Lin-Manuel may have left the cast of *Hamilton*, but he hasn't stopped singing, acting, and writing songs. He wrote songs for the Disney film *Moana*. He had a starring role in the film *Mary Poppins Returns*. And he'll be working on the music for a live-action version of *The Little Mermaid*.

He continues to do everything he can to celebrate Latino culture and share that with the world. He also helps raise money for Puerto Rico and for important causes like women's health.

What else is in store for one of Broadway's most popular stars ever? Whatever it is, we know that Lin-Manuel will change the world with his art. He'll turn to his friends for help and work hard to make his dreams come true.

Now that you've met him, don't you think you can do the same?

BUT WAIT . . .

THERE'S MORE!

Turn the page to read a time line about Puerto Rico, discover some interesting facts about Broadway, and learn how to write your own play!

History of Puerto Rico

Lin-Manuel Miranda's family is from Puerto Rico, an island in the Caribbean Sea. Read this time line to learn about major events in Puerto Rico's history!

1000 C.E.: The Taino people live in Puerto Rico, which they call Boriquén. They eat cassava, which is a tropical root plant. They also eat sweet potatoes and seafood.

November 19, 1493: Christopher Columbus lands on the island and claims it for the Spanish king and queen.

1521: The Spanish explorer Ponce de León establishes a harbor named Puerto Rico, or "Rich Port." Over time, the name of the harbor changes to San Juan. The entire island becomes known as Puerto Rico.

1600s: San Juan becomes a military post for the Spanish army. The native people earn money by trading sugarcane, ginger, and cattle.

December 10, 1898: Spain loses the Spanish-American War and gives Puerto Rico to the United States. Puerto Ricans become U.S. citizens, but they aren't allowed to vote or choose their leaders.

October 1950: U.S. President Harry Truman signs the Puerto Rico Commonwealth Bill, which allows Puerto Ricans to have their own constitution and elect their own governor.

Today: Puerto Rico is still a commonwealth, but some people want it to become the fifty-first state of America. Others want Puerto Rico to become its own country.

Broadway by the Numbers

Become a Broadway theater expert with
these fun facts and figures.

- Broadway is a group of forty theaters in New York that are mainly used for plays and musicals. A play is a performance that tells the story through speech. A musical tells the story through both singing and talking.

- Broadway shows usually have eight performances each week.

- Only five theaters are actually located on the street named Broadway! The bulk of the theaters are located on side streets that cross Broadway.

- In the 2016–2017 season, people went to a Broadway show thirteen million times.

• The longest running Broadway show is *The Phantom of the Opera*.

• The Tony Awards are like the Oscars for Broadway. There are twenty-six award categories, including "Best Costume Design of a Play" and "Best Direction of a Musical."

• *Hamilton* holds the record for the most Tony nominations ever—sixteen.

• *West Side Story* has been produced five different times on Broadway. Lin-Manuel Miranda worked on the fifth production. The show has also toured America two times.

Write Your Own Play

Write your own play script by following these simple steps. Maybe someday you, too, will become a Broadway writer!

First brainstorm **ideas** about the story of the play. Do you want it to be nonfiction (a story that took place in real life) or fiction (something you make up yourself)? Will it be funny, spooky, sad, or happy? Where should it take place?

Next it's time to think about the **characters**. Are they human or not? How do the characters know one another? If you're stuck, try reading biographies of famous people—that's how Lin-Manuel decided to write *Hamilton*!

Just like this book has chapters, or parts, a play can be divided into different **scenes**. How many scenes do you want your play to have?

Now you're ready to write. Plays are made up of **dialogue** and **stage directions**. Dialogue, or speaking lines, are the words that the characters say out loud. Stage directions are included

for the actors and actresses. They describe an action, a character's feelings, or any other important information. The dialogue and stage directions are written in this style.

LIN-MANUEL
(pointing off stage)
Look at that dog!

(TOBILLO approaches VANESSA,
sniffing her feet.)

VANESSA
Where is the owner?

LIN-MANUEL
(worried)
Maybe she's a stray dog. She looks really
hungry.

VANESSA
(laughing)
She's hungry enough to try
to eat my ankle!

Those are all the basics you need for writing a play. If you want to make a musical like Lin-Manuel Miranda did, you can include song lyrics in your play too. Don't forget to add a title. Congratulations—now you're a playwright!

Now that you've met Lin-Manuel, what have you learned?

1. Where were Lin-Manuel's parents born?

a. Puerto Rico
b. Florida
c. New York

2. According to Lin-Manuel, who helped him gain good taste in music?

a. his mom
b. his sister
c. his drama teacher

3. When Lin-Manuel was younger, how did he memorize song lyrics?

a. He wrote the lyrics down.

b. He listened to the songs many times.

c. He made dance moves to the songs.

4. What languages does Lin-Manuel speak?

a. English and Spanish
b. English and Hindi
c. English and Latin

5. What show did Lin-Manuel write in college?

a. *The Electric Company*
b. *In the Heights*
c. *Washington's Story*

6. What is the name of Lin-Manuel's freestyle rap group?

a. Alexander Hamilton
b. Rapping for All
c. Freestyle Love Supreme

7. Why did Lin-Manuel choose hip-hop for *Hamilton*?

a. He thought Broadway music was boring.

b. Hip-hop is energetic and exciting.

c. Alexander Hamilton liked hip-hop.

8. What happened after Lin-Manuel sang at the White House?

a. Lin-Manuel appeared on *Sesame Street*.

b. President Obama asked for an autograph.

c. Everyone watched the video on YouTube.

9. Why is Lin-Manuel's dog named Tobillo?

a. The dog nibbled Vanessa's ankle, and Tobillo means "ankle" in Spanish.

b. Tobillo means "dog" in Spanish.

c. It rhymes with Lin-Manuel's middle name.

10. What is NOT a reason why Lin-Manuel chose actors and actresses of color for *Hamilton*?

a. He wanted to work with the same cast as *In the Heights*.

b. He wanted the cast to look like America today.

c. He wanted to celebrate the people who get left out of history books.

Answers: 1.a 2.b 3.b 4.a 5.b 6.c 7.b 8.c 9.a 10.a

REPRODUCIBLE